Essentials of Data Engineering

Create a solid data system plan and build

Koso Brown

Introduction

Since the early Roman era, data has been an integral aspect of human identity. We ran into scale problems during the US census of 1880 as a result of our growing interconnectedness. From 0% of the globe to 59.5% of the world is now online. An enormous amount of data is generated by the 4.32 billion people who own smartphones. How has humanity responded to the necessity of analyzing this vastly unheard-of volume of data? In an attempt to control this torrent of 1s and 0s, we have devised punch cards, relational databases, the cloud, Hadoop, distributed computing, and even real-time stream processing.

Many people naturally associate computers and pipelines with the concept of data engineering. However, data and the idea of data engineering are not new. Similar to many computer-driven pipelines today, the human-driven pipelines of the pre-computer era had extremely poor SLAs and several problems with data quality.

In English, the word "data" was originally used in the 1640s. The term back then was "a fact given or granted." The fact that the current definition is "potentially sketchy byte value in a computer," I'm sure would have startled folks back then.

Chapter 1 What is Data Engineering?

Making unprocessed data useful for data scientists and other groups inside an organization is a difficult task known as "data engineering." Data science includes a wide range of specializations, including data engineering.

Data engineers make data available and produce raw data analytics that yield prediction models and illustrate both short- and long-term trends. Making sense of the massive volumes of data businesses have access to would only be possible with data engineering.

Large organizations typically have a wide variety of operations management software, such as production systems, ERP, CRM, and others, all of which contain databases with a variety of data. Furthermore, data can be instantly retrieved from external sources, like Internet of Things devices, or saved as distinct files. Running analytics and getting a clear picture of the organization's business situation are hampered by data that is dispersed across many formats.

The process of data engineering

The process of data engineering involves a series of steps that transform a substantial volume of unprocessed data into a useful product that can be used by analysts, data scientists, machine learning engineers, and other professionals. The following steps are usually included in an end-to-end workflow.

In summary, a data engineering procedure.

- ❖ Data serving: is the process of delivering converted data to end consumers, such as a data science team, dashboard, or BI platform.

- ❖ Data ingestion (acquisition): transfers information to a target system for transformation in preparation for additional analysis from a variety of sources, including websites, streaming services, IoT devices, SQL and NoSQL databases, and more. There are many different types of data, and it can be organized or unorganized.

❖ Data transformation: it modifies heterogeneous data to meet end-user requirements. It entails normalizing the data, eliminating errors and duplication, and transforming it into the required format.

Pipeline for data engineering

The process of moving data from one system to another for archiving and additional processing is called a data pipeline. Data engineers are primarily responsible for building and managing data pipelines. They create scripts to automate jobs and other repetitive processes, among other things.

The most common uses of pipelines include
❖ tables being copied between databases.

❖ data integration between different IoT devices and platforms;

❖ processing raw data to create a format that may be used for analytics, business intelligence, and machine learning applications;

❖ data transfer between settings or systems (from

on-site databases to cloud databases)

ETL pipeline

The most popular architecture, which has been around for decades, is the ETL (Extract, Transform, Load) pipeline. An ETL developer is a specialized specialist who frequently implements it.

The following procedures are automated via an ETL pipeline, as the name implies.

1.   Extract means to retrieve info. We work with raw data from multiple sources at the beginning of the pipeline, including files, databases, and APIs.

2.   Standardize data by transforming it. After data is extracted, scripts modify it to fit the specified format. Data transformation greatly enhances the usefulness and discoverability of data.

3.   Loading involves storing data at a new location. Once data is ready for use, engineers can load it into the target, which is usually a data warehouse or database management system (DBMS).

Chapter 2 ETL processes

Following its transformation and loading into a centralized repository, the data can be utilized for business intelligence tasks such as report generation, visualization creation, and more. The expert carrying out ETL pipelines

The ELT pipelines

The steps in an ELT pipeline are Extract, Load, and Transform, however, they are done in a different order. Rather than converting all the gathered data, you store it in a data lake, warehouse, or lakehouse. It can be entirely or partially processed and formatted later, once or multiple times.

When you want to absorb as much data as possible and alter it later, based on new requirements, ELT pipelines are the best option. The ELT architecture does not need you to choose data types and formats ahead of time, in contrast to ETL. Both traditional and real-time analytics are frequently made possible in large-scale projects by combining two different types of data pipelines. In order to facilitate Big Data analytics, two designs may also be used.

Problems with the data pipeline
It can be difficult to set up a trustworthy and secure data flow. There are numerous ways that data transportation might go wrong, including data corruption, bottlenecks that cause slowness, and conflicts between data sources that result in duplicate or inaccurate data. To get all the data in one location, meticulous preparation and testing are needed to weed out irrelevant information, remove duplicates, and deal with incompatible data types so that private information is hidden without being lost.

Building data pipelines can involve two key pitfalls:

❖ absent pertinent metrics

❖ underestimate the amount of data.

NB: A robust and pertinent metrics system is essential because it can tell us about the state and performance of each pipeline stage while underestimating the amount of data it has to process. By this, I mean that the system should be designed so that it won't overload in the event that the product sees an unanticipated spike in user demand.

Chapter 3 Data warehouse

A data warehouse (DW) is a central location where quarriable data is kept. Technically speaking, a data warehouse is a relational database designed to read, aggregate, and query massive amounts of data. Table-based or structured data was the sole kind of data that DWs held in the past. All unstructured data, including pictures, PDFs, and audio files, can be supported by contemporary DWs, though.

Without data warehouses (DWs), data scientists would have to extract data directly from the production database, which could lead to discrepancies in the answers to the same queries or even delays and outages. The data warehouse, which functions as an organization's single source of truth, streamlines decision-making, metrics forecasting, and reporting and analysis inside the company.

DW isn't your typical database, which is surprising. In what way then?

They vary in terms of data structure first. A normalized

database separates similar data into tables and eliminates redundancies in the data. Because a single query aggregates data from numerous tables, this requires a significant amount of processing power. Instead, a DW leverages a small number of tables and straightforward queries to boost analytics and speed.

Second, because they are designed for daily transactions, normal transactional databases typically don't keep historical data; however, warehouses do, since they gather information over an extended period of time. The work of a data analyst is made easier by DW, which enables the manipulation of all data from a single interface and the creation of statistics, analytics, and visualizations.

A database intended for a small group of analysts and decision-makers typically supports more concurrent users than a data warehouse.

Four key elements are combined to build a data warehouse.

Data warehouse management instruments:

The data warehouse handles several administrative and managerial tasks for the entire company. To this end, there are solutions specifically designed for managing data warehouses.

Metadata: Metadata helps turn data into understandable knowledge by providing it with business context. The processing and modification of data are defined by metadata. When source data is loaded into the data warehouse, it contains details on any modifications or activities made to it.

Data warehouse access instruments: The functions of these instruments differ. For instance, business analysis reports are produced using query and reporting technologies. Furthermore, data mining technologies use sophisticated statistical modeling approaches to automatically identify patterns and connections in massive volumes of data.

Storage in a data warehouse: All enterprise data is stored in a database, which forms the basis of data warehouse architecture and is accessible by business users for insightful analysis.

Data architects typically choose between DWs hosted in the cloud and on-premises while considering the advantages each solution may offer the company. In terms of query speed and security, on-premise systems may prevail over cloud environments, despite the latter's greater affordability, ease of scaling up or down, and lack of adherence to a set structure. Later on, we will enumerate the most widely used tools.

For your data warehouse, a data architect can also create collective storage, which consists of several databases operating simultaneously. As a result, the warehouse will be more scalable.

A big advancement in improving your data architecture is a data warehouse. But if you have hundreds of users across several departments, DWs may become too heavy and slow to utilize. Data marts can be developed and put into use in this situation to boost productivity.

Data marts

Simple data warehouses that concentrate on a specific topic or industry are called data marts. Teams who use a data mart save time by not having to manually aggregate data from several sources or search through a more complex data warehouse, allowing them to access data and obtain insights more quickly.

To put it simply, a data mart is a smaller data warehouse—typically, they are fewer than 100 gigabytes in size. When a company grows and its data volume increases, they become essential since it takes too long and is no longer efficient to search for information in an enterprise data warehouse. Rather, data marts are designed to facilitate rapid and easy access to essential information for many departments, including as sales, marketing, and the C-suite.

Chapter 4 Why create a data mart?

Within your company, a data mart makes it simpler to retrieve the data needed by a particular team or business unit. Sorting through and merging data that is dispersed across several systems, for instance, could be expensive in terms of time, accuracy, and money if your marketing team is searching for information to enhance campaign effectiveness over the holiday season.

Spreadsheets are the most common tool used by teams who have to find data from multiple sources and then share it in order to work together. The so-called "spreadsheet nightmare" is typically the result, resulting in human mistake, confusion, intricate reconciliations, and many sources of truth. As a central location for gathering and organizing the relevant data prior to creating reports, dashboards, and visualizations, data marts have gained popularity.

- ❖ **Hybrid data marts:** consolidate data from operational systems and DW systems.

It is therefore difficult to execute and manage queries in a data warehouse (DW), which is a huge repository that holds all firm data derived from many sources. This is the major distinction between a data mart and a data warehouse. On the other hand, a data mart is a condensed repository that holds a restricted quantity of data for a certain department or business unit.

- ❖ **Dependent data marts:** are produced from an enterprise data warehouse and utilized as the main information source (sometimes referred to as a top-down method).
- ❖ **Independent data marts:** are stand-alone systems that work without data wranglers (DWs) by gathering data from a variety of internal and external sources (sometimes referred to as a top-down method).

Chapter 5 A data mart's advantages

There are various advantages to having a data mart

devoted to a certain team or industry:

- ❖ Creating data management that is scalable and agile. Using information from previous projects to assist with current duties is only one of the many ways that data marts offer an agile data management solution that adapts to business demands. Based on new and developing analytics projects, teams can update and modify their data mart.

- ❖ Momentary examination. Completing a particular study of online sales for a two-week campaign before a team meeting is an example of a short-lived data analytics assignment. To complete a project like this, teams can quickly set up a data mart.

- ❖ Simpler and more quickly to deploy. A large amount of time and work may go into setting up an enterprise data warehouse to meet the demands of your whole company. A data mart, on the other hand, needs access to fewer data sets because it is concentrated on meeting the needs of particular business teams. As such, it is easier and quicker to deploy.

❖ An exclusive source of reality. Everyone in a department or organization may make decisions based on the same data thanks to a data mart's centralized structure. This has several advantages, including the ability for stakeholders to concentrate on making decisions and acting rather than debating the data itself and the reliability of the data and the forecasts made with it.

❖ Quicker decision-making due to quicker insights. Department-level data analytics are possible with a data mart, while enterprise-level decision-making is enabled by a data warehouse. Analysts are able to make better and quicker decisions by focusing on particular possibilities and challenges in fields like finance and HR and moving more quickly from data to insights.

❖ Faster data accessibility. The enterprise data warehouse enables users and specific business teams to quickly retrieve the subset of data they require and merge it with data from multiple other sources. They won't need to visit IT to get recurring extracts because they can get real-time data from a data mart whenever needed once the links to their preferred data sources are made. As a result, both IT and business teams experience increased productivity.

Although data marts facilitate prompt access to query data for business users, information alone is frequently insufficient. To obtain useful insights that aid in decision-making, it must be efficiently processed and analyzed. With the help of OLAP cubes, you can examine your data from several angles. Let's examine them.

Chapter 6 OLAP as well as OLAP cubes

Online Analytical Processing, or OLAP, is the computational methodology that enables users to examine multidimensional data. It is in contrast to Online Transaction Processing (OLTP), a fewer complex means of communicating with databases that aren't intended for large-scale data analysis from many angles. Because they use a two-dimensional structure consisting of rows and columns, traditional databases resemble spreadsheets. On the other hand, datasets are shown as multidimensional OLAP cubes. These structures allow large amounts of diverse data to be processed efficiently and subjected to sophisticated analysis. A sales department report, for instance, might contain details about the product, region, sales representative, number of sales, month, and so forth.

The OLAP cube receives aggregated data from DWs and loads it, precalculating and making the data easily accessible to users upon request.

OLAP allows for the analysis of data from several angles. If you need to alter the data representation hierarchy level and obtain a more or less detailed image, for instance, it can be rolled up or drilled down. Additionally, you can dice the data to make a new cube or slice it to divide it into distinct spreadsheets for a certain dataset. These and other methods make it possible to identify trends in a variety of data and generate a broad range of reports.

The fact that OLAP cubes need to be created specifically for each report and analytical query should not be overlooked. But as we mentioned, they make it possible to do sophisticated, multidimensional analysis that was previously too difficult, therefore their use is acceptable.

The Importance of Data Engineering

Businesses gather data in order to improve corporate procedures and comprehend market trends. The basis for evaluating the effectiveness of various tactics and solutions is data, which helps to more precisely and effectively drive growth.

The big data analytics industry is expected to develop at a compound annual growth rate (CAGR) of 13.5% from its estimated valuation of USD 271.83 billion in 2022 to USD 745.15 billion by 2030. The information demonstrates the significance of data engineering and the rising demand for its worldwide.

Data engineers facilitate the data collection process, which in turn facilitates the reliable analysis of the available data by scientists, executives, and data analysts. An essential function of data engineering is in:

- ❖ Assembling data using several data integration tools in one location
- ❖ Strengthening the security of information
- ❖ Safeguarding businesses from cyberattacks
- ❖ Supplying optimal procedures to improve the complete cycle of product development

Data pipelines and ETL (Extract, Transform, Load) procedures are among the main reasons data engineering is important. In order to guarantee that data is gathered, cleaned, transformed, and made accessible to data scientists, analysts, and other stakeholders in an organized and trustworthy manner, data engineers design, construct, and maintain these pipelines. This permits easy access to data, enabling teams to get insightful information and take well-informed decisions that propel efficiency and success in the organization.

Data engineering, to put it briefly, makes sure that data is consistent, coherent, and complete.

Data Engineering for Integrity and Quality of Data

In data quality management, data engineering is also essential. By putting strict data governance procedures into place, data engineers ensure that the data is accurate, consistent, and comprehensive. Through adherence to best practices and careful curation of data, they assist sustain a high degree of data trustworthiness, facilitating confident decision-making throughout the business. Furthermore, performance and scalability depend on data engineering. To manage and analyze data effectively, businesses need strong infrastructure and optimum data storage solutions as the volume of data increases. In order to ensure seamless operations even in the face of a large data influx, data engineers create data architectures that can scale to meet growing data needs.

Security and compliance are also top priorities for companies handling sensitive data. Data engineers play a crucial role in putting industry regulations into practice, enforcing data security measures, and protecting the confidentiality and privacy of data.

Data engineering is a key enabler in the age of AI and advanced analytics. In order to transform data into predictive and prescriptive insights that spur innovation and competitive advantage, data engineers work in tandem with data scientists to develop data models and apply machine learning algorithms.

To put it briefly, data engineering is essential for today's businesses because it serves as the foundation for efficient data management, quality control, scalability, security, and the incorporation of cutting-edge technology. Firms that allocate resources towards strong data engineering competencies situate themselves to leverage their data resources, attain a competitive advantage, and prosper in an era driven by data.

Chapter 7 Big Data Engineering

Big Data is a topic we cannot overlook while discussing data engineering. It typically inundates major tech corporations like YouTube, Amazon, or Instagram. It is based on the four Vs: volume, velocity, variety, and veracity. Big Data engineering involves creating extremely scalable, fault-tolerant distributed systems and large reservoirs.

Because we're dealing with enormous volumes of constantly changing data streams that a data warehouse cannot hold, big data architecture is different from traditional data management. A data lake can be useful in this situation.

Data lake

An enormous reservoir for storing data in its original, raw form is called a data lake. Its exceptional agility comes from the fact that it isn't constrained by the fixed layout of a warehouse.

When managing raw, frequently unstructured data, a data lake employs the ELT methodology and begins data loading right away after extraction.

For projects that will grow and require a more sophisticated design, it makes sense to establish a data lake. Additionally, it is highly practical in situations where the data's intended use is still unknown. This allows you to swiftly load data, store it, and make any necessary modifications.

For data scientists and ML engineers who would use raw data to prepare it for machine learning and predictive analytics, data lakes are also an effective tool.

Large, dispersed clusters that can handle and store enormous amounts of data are the foundation upon which lakes are created. Hadoop is a well-known illustration of a data lake platform.

The data engineer's role

After learning about the scope of data engineering, let's examine the position of a data engineer, who specializes in developing software solutions centered around large data.

"Assure the availability and quality of data is the primary responsibility of the data engineer in a multidisciplinary team comprising data scientists, BI engineers, and data engineers." It also involves the possibility of a data engineer working in tandem with other professionals to develop or implement a data-related feature (or product), such as an A/B test, a machine learning model, or the improvement of an already-existing data source.

Skills and qualifications

There is overlap in skills since data engineering is the area where software engineering and data science converge.

- ❖ Systems creation skills. Building data pipelines requires data engineers to have knowledge with a variety of data storage systems and frameworks.

- ❖ Data-related skills. Data platforms, MapReduce, batch and stream processing, various database types (including SQL and NoSQL), and even some fundamental data theory, such as data types and descriptive statistics, should all be understood by a data engineer.

❖ Software engineering background. To provide dependable and practical access to data and databases, data engineers employ programming languages. Juan highlights that they are capable of working with all phases of the software development life cycle, which includes developing metrics, defining them, prototyping, testing, deployment, and DevOps. Experienced programmers, at least in Python or Scala/Java, are data engineers.

Toolkit

To select the appropriate data technologies for a given task, a data engineer needs to possess a thorough understanding of a wide range of data technologies.

Big data tools. Data lakes, Hadoop and its ecosystem, Elastic Stack for end-to-end big data analytics, and more are technologies that a data engineer should be proficient in, or at least aware of.

Warehouse solutions. On-premise data warehouse solutions that are often utilized include Oracle Exadata, IBM db2, SAP Data Warehouse, Teradata Data Warehouse, and IBM db2. Amazon Redshift and Google BigQuery are the two most widely used cloud-based data warehousing technologies.

Cloud Dataflow. On-premise data warehouse solutions that are often utilized include Oracle Exadata, IBM db2, SAP Data Warehouse, Teradata Data Warehouse, and IBM db2. Amazon Redshift and Google BigQuery are the two most widely used cloud-based data warehousing technologies.

Airflow. Airbnb built this Python-based workflow management solution to rebuild its data pipeline architecture. The organization cut the run-time of their experimental reporting framework (ERF) from more than 24 hours to roughly 45 minutes after migrating to Airflow. Juan lists the operators' ability to "execute bash commands, run a SQL query, or even send an email" as one of the advantages of Airflow. Juan also highlights the complete and extensive user interface, the project's general maturity, and Airflow's capacity to deliver Slack notifications. Conversely, Airflow restricts job writing to Python alone.

Chapter 8 Data engineer vs data scientist

While they both use data, "data scientists and data engineers solve quite different tasks, have different skills, and use different tools," Massive data storage is created and maintained by data engineers, who also use engineering skills including database languages, ETL procedures, computer languages, and familiarity with various data warehouses. On the other hand, data scientists use their machine learning tools and algorithms, math and algorithmic skills, and data cleaning and analysis skills to extract important insights from the data and apply models for forecasting and predictive analytics.

Data Engineers' Responsibilities

A data engineer is a person who designs, builds, tests, and maintains large-scale processing systems and databases, among other structures. The person who cleans, manipulates, and arranges (huge) data is known as a data scientist.

Although the verb "massage" may seem like a

particularly unusual choice to you, it only highlights even more of the distinction between data scientists and data engineers.

To put it generally, getting the data in a format that can be used will require a lot of work on the part of both parties.

Raw data containing flaws from humans, machines, or instruments is what data engineers work with. The data may be unformatted, contain codes that are peculiar to a certain system, and contain records that are not verified.

It will be up to the data engineers to suggest and occasionally carry out improvements to data quality, efficiency, and dependability. For example, in order to convert system-specific codes into information that data scientists can use for additional processing, they will need to use a range of languages and tools to marry systems together or look for chances to obtain fresh data from other systems.

The fact that data engineers must make sure the

architecture in place satisfies the needs of the stakeholders—the business and data scientists—and these two is intimately tied to each other.

Finally, in order to provide the data to the data science team, the data engineering team must create data set procedures for data mining, production, and modeling.

For data scientists, accessing data can be challenging for a number of reasons.

* Different APIs are available to access different data repositories. Data engineers are necessary for data scientists to build the most dependable and effective data acquisition pipeline.
* Data is typically kept in a variety of formats and systems. It makes logical to start with data preparation and transfer information to a central repository, such as a data warehouse. Usually, data architects and engineers are responsible for this.
* To access and handle large volumes of data in a suitable length of time, extra work and specialized engineering solutions are needed.

Data Scientists' Responsibilities

When preparing data for use in predictive and prescriptive modeling, data scientists can utilize advanced analytics tools, machine learning, and statistical techniques. Typically, they are provided with data that has already undergone some initial cleaning and manipulation. Naturally, they must conduct industry and business research before developing models, and in order to meet business requirements, they must make use of vast amounts of data from both internal and external sources. In order to uncover hidden patterns, this occasionally also entails analyzing and investigating data.

Upon completion of the analyses, data scientists must clearly communicate their findings to the important stakeholders. If the results are approved, they must then ensure that the work is automated to enable daily, monthly, or annual delivery of the insights to the business stakeholders.

It is obvious that in order to go through the data and offer insights for decisions that are crucial to the business, both sides must collaborate. Although the two roles clearly overlap, the data scientist must be knowledgeable in statistics, math, and machine learning in order to create predictive models. The data engineer, on the other hand, will work with database systems, data APIs, and tools for ETL purposes, as well as data modeling and setting up data warehouse solutions.

In addition to needing to access the data that the data engineering team has processed, the data scientist must be knowledgeable of distributed computing in order to effectively communicate to the business stakeholders. Storytelling and visual aids are crucial in this regard.

Conclusion

In the last several years, there has been a sharp rise in the demand for data engineers. Data engineers are in demand by businesses to handle their data needs. Optimizing and making use of data is the core of data engineering. Data engineers must thus constantly learn new tools and keep up with the latest developments in their field. Data engineering is unquestionably the best career choice for someone who wants to work with enormous amounts of data.

A growing number of enterprises are using data engineering tools in response to the data overload that many faces as they transition to digital processes.